Once Upon a Time

Written by Cass Hollander

Illustrated by Angela Adams

"Once upon a time, there was a stone."

 "No, no, no! Tell a good story. Don't tell a story about a stone."

"Okay. Once upon a time, there were three bears."

 "That's good. Tell me more."

"The three bears went for a ride on their bikes."

"No, no, no! They went for a walk."

"Okay. They went for a walk. On the way, they wanted to see Grandma."

"No, no, no! They did not want to see Grandma. They just went for a walk. Tell about the girl at their house."

"Okay. When the bears went for a walk, a girl went into their house. She made some good food."

"No, no, no! The girl went in and ate the food."

"Okay. The girl tried one bowl of food, but it was much too hot. She tried one bowl of food, but it was much too cold. She tried the last bowl of food, but she heard someone at the door."

"It was a wolf!"

 "No, no, no! You're all mixed up! This is not a good story."

"Okay. Then the bears came back. The girl and the wolf ran to hide."

13

"The three bears saw them. The three bears thought the girl and the wolf wanted to play hide and seek. They went to find them."

"The girl, the wolf, and the three bears played hide and seek all day. And I think they lived happily ever after."

15

"That was a good story! Now can you tell me one about three pigs?"